Chakras & Weight Loss

Debby Ng

Waitloss Journeys

Introduction
Unveiling the Energetic Map of Well-Being

Aloha and welcome to this transformative journey where the ancient wisdom of chakras intertwines with the modern pursuit of well-being and weight loss. Chakras, the energy centers within our subtle bodies, have been a part of spiritual traditions for centuries, guiding individuals towards balance, vitality, and harmony.

Understanding the Chakras: An Energetic Blueprint

Chakras, derived from the Sanskrit word for "wheel," represent the spinning vortexes of energy that align along the spine. In total, there are seven main chakras, each associated with distinct qualities and aspects of our being, creating an energetic blueprint that shapes our physical, emotional, and spiritual well-being.

- Root Chakra (Muladhara): Grounding and stability.
- Sacral Chakra (Swadhisthana): Creativity and passion.
- Solar Plexus Chakra (Manipura): Personal power and confidence.
- Heart Chakra (Anahata): Love and compassion.
- Throat Chakra (Vishuddha): Communication and self-expression.
- Third Eye Chakra (Ajna): Intuition and insight.
- Crown Chakra (Sahasrara): Spiritual connection and higher consciousness.

The Unseen Impact: Chakras and Emotional Blocks

For many, the knowledge of chakras is familiar, but the profound realization often comes when we understand how these energy centers can hold the imprints of our life experiences, especially trauma. It's not merely a metaphysical concept but a tangible map of the emotional and spiritual landscape within us.

In my personal journey, I always sensed the subtle currents of energy but never fully grasped their significance until I discovered the intricate link between chakras and emotional blocks. It was an awakening—an understanding that the energetic imbalances within could manifest as physical weight and emotional baggage.

Overview of Our Chakras:

Root Chakra Unveiled 🌱🔴

Welcome to the powerhouse of earthly vibes – the Root Chakra, aka Muladhara! 🌏✨ This bad boy sets up camp near the perineum, anchoring us to the very essence of our existence on this beautiful planet.

Picture this: Muladhara is the CEO of grounding, the maestro of deep connection with our environment. 🌿🌍 It's like plugging into the Earth's Wi-Fi, soaking in that delicious, stabilizing energy. Safety and grounding become its anthem, creating a fortress of stability for your cosmic journey.

Why the fancy name, Muladhara? Well, it's got that feminine energy, a real queen of the chakra realm. 👑✨ And boy, does it have a vast empire to rule – think lower back, lower spine, kidneys, and bladder. Muladhara is the CEO of the lower body, making sure everything down there is working like a well-oiled machine.

Let's dive into the Root Chakra's greatest hits: family, physical energy, survival, courage, stability, and material matters. 💪💼 Passion and love? Oh, it's got those in its playlist too, set to the soulful note of 'C' and wrapped in the vibrant hues of red, the color of passion and vital force.

And now, introducing the entourage of gems that rock its world: ruby red, red garnet, rhodochrosite, red jasper, red carnelian, black tourmaline, and obsidian – the A-listers of the crystal kingdom. 💎✨

Ready to strike a pose? Meet the Yoga Posse: Mountain, Squat, Warrior, Goddess, and Child's Pose – the superheroes of Muladhara activation. Or take it to the streets with a barefoot walking meditation, recharging your energy straight from the Earth's core.

So, dear Earth-dwellers, embrace the roots, feel the vibes, and dance to the rhythm of your Muladhara magic. 🌱🎶 #RootChakraMagic #GroundedGlow #ChakraConnection

Root Chakra Prescription 💚🕯️

Listen up, cosmic navigators! Your Root Chakra, the Muladhara maestro, has some insider insights for you. 🌱🌟

Body Talk: If your vessel feels a bit wonky, it's like your body's SOS signal. Maybe those basic needs aren't getting the attention they deserve. Check the vibes – excessive energy with the chakra on turbo mode might lead to some not-so-zen vibes like aggression and a touch of egotism. On the flip side, if it's spinning in slow-mo, that could spell out a lack of confidence, weak willpower, and a bit of a disconnect from the groove of life.

Essential Elixirs: Time to bring in the A-team of aromas! Earthy essential oils and the cosmic trio of sandalwood, cedarwood, cloves, and ginger are your chakra's BFFs. Imagine them as scented guardians, wrapping you in a cocoon of grounding goodness. Light up those candles

or incense, and let the aroma symphony begin.
🕯️ ✨

Mantras to the Rescue: Affirmations are like verbal spells for your soul. Repeat after me: "I am here. I am safe. I am nourished. I am supported by Mother Earth." Feel that? Now, take a deep breath and release the anxiety and fear within. Let the earth cradle you in its support. You're not just in your body; you're at home in it. 🌍💚

So, fellow Earthlings, nurture your roots, find your groove, and let the Muladhara magic flow. 🌱🔮 #RootChakraRevival #EssentialAlchemy #ChakraAffirmations

Sacral Symphony 🌊🧡

Dive into the waves of the Sacral Chakra, Svadhisthana – your gateway to the ocean of emotions, pleasure, and creativity. 🌊✨ Nestled just below the navel, it's the heart of relationships, desire, and the cosmic dance of the waters.

Chakra 411: Picture this chakra as your emotional compass, guiding you through the realms of pleasure, relationships, and creativity. It's the groove of water, the ebb and flow of emotions, and the pulsing rhythm of life. 🔮💖

Harmony Hues: Picture a palette of orange – the color of carnelian and modern citrine. It's like sunshine for your soul. 🌇🧡 And when the cosmic orchestra plays the note 'D,' it's time to dance to the rhythm of your own emotions.

Life's Dance Floor: This chakra isn't just a step; it's the first dance on your ladder of consciousness. Imbalances? Watch out for bladder and kidney hiccups, circulation conundrums, and the occasional migraine. Too much juice in this chakra might lead to aggression and overindulgence, while a shortage could brew guilt and resentment.

Sacral Chakra Prescriptions🧡 🕯️

Soul Serenades: Affirmations, your soul's power chords. Repeat after me: "I am living a pleasurable life. I have complete peace from within. I trust my feelings and give them ample room for expression. I allow my creativity to flow through me freely." Feel that sweet symphony resonate within. 🎶🌸

Balance Beats: Clear the emotional clutter! Write down past emotional baggage on notes, throw them away, and let your past emotions evaporate with the notes. Feel the lightness that follows.

Healing Elixirs: Aromatherapy to the rescue! Cardamom, eucalyptus, chamomile, spearmint, rose, or clarity sage – they're the healers in your essential oils toolkit. Let them restore sensuality and unleash your creative muse. 

Crystal Allies: Open up with orange and coral calcite, carnelian, or citrine. Feeling overwhelmed? Amber's got your back – soothing and healing vibes for days. 💎 🔮

Yoga Bliss: Let mindful breathing serenade your soul while diving into yoga poses like bound angle, squat, goddess, and happy baby. Feel the energies flow and dance within.

Fluid Connection: Water is the name of the game. Swim, sit by a flowing stream, or soak in a relaxing bath. And don't forget the creative expression – coloring, drawing, cooking, baking, or gardening – let the creativity flow like a river. So, beloved ocean dwellers, let the Sacral Chakra serenade your soul. 🌊 🌈

#SacralSerenity #ChakraMagic #CreativeFlow

Solar Plexus Unleashed 🔥💛

Step into the radiant realm of the Solar Plexus, ManiPura – your powerhouse for momentum and realizing desires. ✨ Nestled at the navel, it's the ignition switch for personal power, identity, and action.

Chakra Chronicles: This chakra isn't just a spot on your stomach; it's your driving force. It's the switch that propels you forward, empowering or weakening your ego along the way. Picture it as the solar light-encoded energy hub, activating nerves that radiate from the pit of your stomach. 💪☀️

Cosmic Colors: In this cosmic dance, yellow takes center stage – the hue of fire, personal power, and intellect. The musical note 'E' sets the rhythm for your nervous system, brain, and the inspiration behind your grand projects.

Digestive Drama: Your body's digestive HQ resides here. Poor digestion? It's the Solar Plexus waving the red flag. Anxiety and fear? The culprits that can throw this chakra off balance. Excessive energy might have you burning the midnight oil, resenting authority, and unleashing the inner judge. Deficient energy? Cue the depression, insecurity, fear of solitude, and a digestive system on strike. Aroma Alchemy: Wake up the Solar Plexus with fiery scents – saffron, musk, sandalwood, ginger, and cinnamon. It's like an olfactory pep talk, stirring the fire within. 🔥🌿

Solar Plexus Chakra Prescriptions 🔥

Mantras of Might: Affirmations, the mantras of your Solar Plexus journey. Repeat after me: "I make my own decisions with confidence and conviction. I give myself permission to be my authentic self. I am motivated to pursue my true purpose. I honor the power within me. I honor myself. The fire within me burns through all blocks and fears." Feel the power surge within.

Crystal Allies: Yellow tourmaline detoxes the body, while amber boosts mental clarity and confidence. Let them be your cosmic companions, balancing and empowering.

Yoga Blaze: Ignite the fiery energy with sun salutations. The boat pose is your ally, strengthening those abdominal muscles and harmonizing digestion.

Healing Harmonies: Traumas, the silent echoes in your body. For Solar Plexus balancing, therapy and support are the guides. When the stomach tightens, try a Taoist meditation – massage clockwise, breathe out stress with big sighs, smile and let it recharge. 🌀🧘‍♂️

So, radiant warriors, let the Solar Plexus blaze. 🔥💛 #SolarPlexusPower #ChakraFire #IgniteYourAuthenticSelf

Heart Chakra Harmony 💚🌸

Step into the center stage of compassion and love – the Heart Chakra, Anahata. 🌿💖 Nestled in the chest, it paints your life with hues of empathy, balance, and the symphony of relationships.

Chakra Symphony: This isn't just a spot in your chest; it's the epicenter of compassion, love, and beauty. Imagine it as a paintbrush, coloring your life with the shades of green – the color of emerald green, green tourmaline, green jasper, and dioptase. Musical note 'F' sets the rhythm for the heart center, health balance, and equanimity.

Cosmic Dance: It's the integrator of the spiritual and earthly realms, blending early aspirations with the cosmic dance of your higher self. This chakra is the maestro of relationships, shaping how you relate to others and handle the dance of connection.

Balance Act: Feeling a bit withdrawn or closed off? Your heart chakra might need a tune-up. Excessive energy might lead to demanding behavior, possessiveness, and a one-way ticket to Moodyville. On the flip side, deficient energy could have you stuck in indecisiveness, fearing rejection, and in constant need of reassurance.

Heart Chakra Prescriptions 💚 🌸

Aroma Alchemy: Infuse your heart with the scents of love – rose, lavender, orange, and jasmine. Let them be the aromatic embrace, opening your heart to the dance of love. 

Mantras of Love: Affirmations, the love notes for your soul. Repeat after me: "I welcome love with an open heart. My heart is free from all wounds of the past. I am open to love, and I receive more of it every day. I am worthy of love. Love is my guiding truth in life. I give and receive love effortlessly and unconditionally." Let the love vibes flow.

Crystal Companions: Rose quartz, the heart healer, aids sleep, calms emotions, and banishes negativity. Jade promotes emotional and physical well-being, while green calcite absorbs negativity and boosts physical immunity.

Yoga Embrace: Let mindful breathing release tension in the heart chakra. Upward facing dog, camel, and bridge poses lift the chest, opening the gates of Anahata.
Heart Balancing Act: The best way to receive love is to give it. Be kinder to others, forgive old grudges, avoid being overly critical, and spread kindness like confetti. 🎉💚

So, radiant souls, let the Heart Chakra dance with compassion and love. 💃💚
#HeartChakraLove #BalancedHarmony #ChakraDance

Throat Chakra Symphony 🔵🎶

Enter the harmonious realm of Vishuddha, the Throat Chakra, where communication and creativity weave the dance of self-expression. 🗣️💙 Nestled in the throat, jaw, neck, and mouth, it orchestrates the flow of energy between the head and the lower body.

Chakra Concerto: Picture this chakra as the cosmic DJ of communication and expression. It's the maestro of the throat, responsible for the thyroid gland and hormonal harmony. As the bridge between the lower body and the head, it's the realm of sound and vibration, containing the essence of all previous elements. Blue Hues of Expression: Blue takes center stage – the color of calm, serenity, and the musical note 'G.' Electric vibes charge the throat with energy. Crystals like cal, aquamarine, celestite, and blue garnet are the cosmic companions.

Balancing Act: When this chakra grooves in balance, we speak openly and authentically, expressing our true selves. Too much energy might lead to overstimulation, arrogance, and dominating conversations. On the flip side, deficiencies could have us hiding opinions, being unreliable, and dancing with manipulation.

Throat Chakra Prescriptions 🔵🎶

Aroma Alchemy: Open the gates with the scents of frankincense, sage, peppermint, and eucalyptus. Let them be the aromatic key unlocking the door to self-expression. 🌿💨

Mantras of Truth: Affirmations, the truth-telling whispers to your soul. Repeat after me: "I hear and speak the truth. I express my love and goodness each time I speak. I love to share my experiences and wisdom. I know when it is time to listen. I listen to my body and my feelings to know what my truth is. I live in my truth. I communicate my truth. I am the truth." Let the truth vibes resonate within.

Crystal Clear Allies: Amazonite promotes emotional balance, turquoise helps express thoughts, and aquamarine clears the mind while encouraging honesty and connecting with hidden emotions.

Yoga Harmonies: Release tensions and let energy flow to the throat with poses like camel, plow, cat-cow with lion's breath, shoulder stand, and fish pose. Feel the liberation in each stretch.

So, cosmic communicators, let the Throat Chakra be your song of self-expression. 🎵💙 #ThroatChakraTune #ExpressYourVibes #ChakraHarmony

Third Eye Symphony 🌀🔮

Step into the cosmic realm between the eyebrows, where insight and intuition dance in harmony – the Third Eye Chakra, Ajna. 🌌💜 Nestled in the space between the eyes, it's the bridge to the pituitary gland, eyes, ears, nose, and the epicenter of light, insight, and vision.

Chakra Cosmos: This isn't just a spot on your forehead; it's the cosmic connection to intuition, dreams, and self-awareness. Indigo is the hue – the color of self-knowledge, blending earth, air, fire, water, and ether. Musical note 'A' sets the rhythm, resonating with sapphire, labradorite, lapis lazuli, and lazuli.

Insightful Insights: A strong Third Eye opens the floodgates of intuition, allowing spiritual growth and a more generous attitude toward life. But, beware! Headaches, eye, and sinus issues might signal a wobbly Third Eye trying to balance everyday activities.

Balancing Act: From the outer world to the inner dialogue, the Third Eye is your cosmic connection. It's the sixth sense, expanding your consciousness. Excessive energy might have you lost in fantasy, while deficiencies could dull your memory and lead to a distrust of your inner voice.

Third Eye Prescriptions 🌀🔮

Aroma Alchemy: Ignite intuition with the scents of bay laurel, palo santo, nutmeg, and Roman chamomile. Let the fragrant wisps awaken the senses within. 🌿✨

Mantras of Insight: Affirmations, the mantras of the Third Eye. Repeat after me: "I am insightful and intuitive. My inner eye reflects my inner light. I am connected with my higher self. I am confident in my ability to make life work. I am worthy of the life I want." Feel the affirmations echo through your being.

Crystal Clear Allies: Amethyst opens, stimulates, and protects. Lapis lazuli balances, while sapphire heals an overactive Third Eye. Let them be the cosmic companions on your journey.

Yoga Visions: Release tension and activate the Third Eye with poses like humble warrior, wide-legged forward bend, locust, camel, dolphin, and child's pose. Feel the energy flow and the cosmic insight unfold.

So, cosmic seers, let the Third Eye unveil the dance of intuition and insight. 🌀🔍 #ThirdEyeWisdom #ChakraInsight #IntuitiveHarmony

Crown Chakra Serenade 👑🌌

Enter the sacred space at the crown of the head, where enlightenment and divine connection dance – the Crown Chakra, Sahasrara. 🌈💫 The pinnacle of the chakra system, it's the gateway to higher selves and the profound understanding that everything is interconnected at a fundamental level.

Chakra Cosmos: This isn't just a spot on your head; it's the cosmic connection to enlightenment, consciousness, and the divine. Violet is the hue – the color of transformation and cosmic energy. Musical note 'B' sets the rhythm, resonating with amethyst, the stone of spiritual wisdom.

Divine Dance: The Crown Chakra dances with key ideas – thought, faith in life, spiritual purpose, wisdom, peace, and oneness. It's the cosmic connection to the universe, the element of cosmic energy embracing all. 🌌🔮

Balancing Act: Beginners might find it intimidating, but with practice, the energy of this chakra strengthens, building a deeper connection to the realm of the divine. Excessive energy may lead to frustration and migraines, while deficiencies can dim the lights of happiness and joy.

Crown Chakra Prescriptions 👑🌌

Aroma Alchemy: Connect with the crown by burning candles, oils, and incense with myrrh, camphor, and frankincense. Let the fragrant wisps elevate your spirit. 🌿

Mantras of Light: Affirmations, the mantras of the Crown Chakra. Repeat after me: "I always trust and follow my intuition. I see divine light in everyone. I am open to the abundance and the greatness the universe offers. I go beyond my limiting beliefs and accept myself totally. I am divine and inspired." Feel the affirmations resonate through the cosmos.

Crystal Celestial Allies: Selenite opens and activates, cleansing the auric field. Clear quartz amplifies energy, heightening spiritual awareness. Amethyst, the meditation maestro, reveals the root cause of imbalance.

Yoga Elevation: To open the crown, meditative poses release tension. Lotus, half lotus, savasana, and tree pose create a sacred space for cosmic connection.
So, cosmic seekers, let the Crown Chakra be your serenade to the divine dance of enlightenment. 👑🌌 #CrownChakraWisdom #DivineConnection #ChakraSerenity

Now that you have learned some things about each chakra and ways to heal, energize and unblock them, let's take an assessment so we can work on one chakra at a time.

Checking Your Chakra Health
A Self-Assessment

Embarking on a journey of self-discovery and healing requires a keen understanding of your chakra system. The chakras, energy centers within your body, play a crucial role in maintaining balance and well-being. To guide you through this exploration, we've crafted a Chakra Health Check—an insightful tool to gauge the vitality of each chakra.

How to Use the Chakra Health Check:

For each chakra, rate the statements on a Likert scale from 1 to 5, where 1 is "Not at all" and 5 is "All the time." Be honest with yourself; this self-assessment is a mirror reflecting your current state of being.

Let's break down the chakras and some sample statements:

<u>First Chakra: Root</u>

- I have trouble finding or holding my ground.
- I'm not at ease in my body.
- I have health challenges.
- I struggle with food, diet, or weight.
- First Chakra Total = ________

...and so on for each chakra.

Interpreting Your Scores:

- All Chakras Total Score = ________

A higher total score may indicate areas of potential improvement, suggesting that your energy centers could benefit from attention and healing. Recognize that this self-assessment is a dynamic tool; as you progress in your journey, retake the quiz to measure your growth and set new goals.

May this Chakra Health Check be a compass on your transformative path, guiding you toward a harmonious and balanced existence.

The Self-Assessment

Rate the statements on a Likert scale from 1 to 5, where 1 is "Not at all" and 5 is "All the time.

First Chakra: Root

_____ I have trouble finding or holding my ground.
_____ I'm not at ease in my body.
_____ I have health challenges.
_____ I hate to exercise.
_____ I struggle with food, diet, or weight.
_____ I never seem to have enough money to live comfortably.
_____ I feel disconnected with nature and the earth.

First Chakra Total = ______

Second Chakra: Sacral
_____ I have trouble knowing what I feel.
_____ Some people think I'm overly emotional.
_____ I find sexuality to be challenging for me.
_____ Life just isn't a whole lot of fun.
_____ My body doesn't move very freely.
_____ I have trouble knowing what I want and need.
_____ If I do know what I want, I'm scared to ask for it.

Second Chakra Total = ______

Third Chakra: Solar Plexus
_____ I get overwhelmed by life's challenges.
_____ I have trouble bringing tasks to completion.
_____ I'm not sure what my purpose is.
_____ I feel intimidated by others.
_____ I struggle with low energy.
_____ I'm not very good at setting boundaries.
_____ My will gets distracted and goes in many directions.

Third Chakra Total = ______

Fourth Chakra: Heart

_____ I have trouble finding or maintaining intimate relationships.
_____ I am critical and judgmental of myself.
_____ I am critical and judgmental of others.
_____ I feel isolated and alone.
_____ I am shy about reaching out.
_____ Other people take too much energy from me.
_____ I hold a lot of grief in my heart.

Fourth Chakra Total = _______

Fifth Chakra: Throat

_____ I have trouble speaking what really matters to me.
_____ I tend to interrupt others when I should be listening.
_____ I have trouble getting my ideas across effectively.
_____ I wish I could be more creative.
_____ I often feel out of sync with others.
_____ I find it difficult to express myself in writing.
_____ Sometimes I don't know what's true in what people tell me.

Fifth Chakra Total = _________

Sixth Chakra: Third Eye

_______ I have trouble trusting my intuition.
_______ I have trouble imagining things different than they are.
_______ Sometimes I ignore that little voice inside.
_______ I rarely remember my dreams.
_______ I don't have a guiding vision for my life.
_______ I have trouble visualizing what I want.
_______ I don't really notice details around me.

Sixth Chakra Total = _________

Seventh Chakra: Crown

_______ I try to meditate but don't stick with it.
_______ I don't feel very connected to any kind of spirituality.
_______ I find it difficult to learn new things.
_______ I often think I'm just not smart enough.
_______ I am wary of new ideas.
_______ I'm not sure of my purpose.
_______ I don't know what I'm here for.

Seventh Chakra Total = _______

<u>Scoring</u>

All Chakras Total Score = _______

"Most of the time" in all columns (worst score) would be 5 x 49 = 245
"Never" in all columns (best score) would be 1 x 49 = 49

If you scored anything between about 100 and 245, it means there's room for improvement.

Turning Struggles into Empowered Goals

The idea is to pick 2 - 3 (at most) items in the assessment preferably in only 1 or 2 chakra areas and create goals.

One way to do this especially to track the results and go deep is to work on one chakra at a time and then measure your assessment again just on that area.

<u>Examples:</u>
Let's delve into showcasing a few areas where individuals might be facing struggles and how these can be transformed into actionable goals:

<u>First Chakra: Root</u> (Scoring 2)
Sarah acknowledges struggling to find her ground and experiencing discomfort in her body. Transforming this into a goal, she sets out to explore grounding practices like daily walks in nature and embracing mindfulness techniques to foster a stronger connection with her physical self. She chooses an essential oil scent for her root chakra and dabs it behind her ears and on her wrists every morning before her walk.

<u>Second Chakra: Sacral</u> (Scoring 3)
Mark recognizes challenges in understanding and expressing his emotions. Embracing growth, his goal becomes delving into practices that enhance emotional intelligence.

Journaling, art, and therapy sessions become integral parts of his journey toward emotional balance. He chooses crystals that represent the sacral chakra and carries them in his pocket to remind him to say his chosen positive affirmations throughout the day.

<u>Fourth Chakra: Heart </u>(Scoring 2)
Scott grapples with maintaining intimate relationships and harboring judgment toward himself and others. As a proactive step, his goal is to foster self-compassion through daily affirmations and cultivating open communication to nurture meaningful connections. He practices these while embracing a rose quartz crystal and standing in the mirror to say I love you to himself, knowing all love starts with self-love.

<u>Fifth Chakra: Throat</u> (Scoring 3)
Emily finds expressing herself challenging, both verbally and in writing. Transitioning this struggle into a goal,

she decides to enroll in a creative writing class and practice mindful communication techniques, allowing her authentic voice to flourish. She carries this practice into journaling and journals while lighting candles which reflect the colors associated with the throat chakra.

<u>Seventh Chakra: Crown</u> (Scoring 2)
Jason expresses uncertainty about his purpose and difficulty in connecting with spirituality. Turning this struggle into a goal, he commits to a daily meditation practice and explores different spiritual philosophies to deepen his connection with higher consciousness. He practices yoga outside in nature when possible and brings crystals often staying in savasana pose for 10-20 minutes taking in inspirations he receives.

By addressing these challenges head-on and framing them as actionable goals, individuals like Sarah, Mark, Scott, Emily, and Jason pave

the way for accelerated self-improvement and a
transformative journey toward holistic
well-being.

Accelerating Growth through Strategic Goal Setting

In the journey toward chakra alignment and holistic well-being, the characters have strategically chosen goals that fall within the 2-3 range on the chakra health scorecard. Opting for these initial challenges allows for a swifter and more tangible sense of progress. By addressing aspects that may not be deeply entrenched, individuals can witness immediate improvements in their daily lives. It's a strategic approach aimed at creating a positive momentum early on, fostering a sense of accomplishment, and setting the stage for more profound transformations. As these characters embark on their self-improvement journeys, the focus on manageable goals serves as a catalyst for growth, laying the groundwork for more profound and lasting changes.

<u>What are your goals for your chakra alignment?</u>

1. ___________________________________

2. ___________________________________

3. ___________________________________

Embracing the Power of I AM: Setting
Intentions for Transformation

In the journey of chakra healing, setting clear intentions becomes a potent catalyst for personal transformation. The "I AM" intention-setting technique invites individuals to envision their desired identities and express them as positive, present-time statements. Take a moment to immerse yourself in the visualization of who you want to be, then distill that vision into a simple and clear "I AM" statement. For example, "I AM alive, vibrant, and full of joy."

Sharing these intentions is a key step in the manifestation process. When declared into the open space of possibility, intentions effortlessly begin to materialize. Whether shared with friends, family, or reflected in the mirror, vocalizing your intentions sends out energetic declarations that align with your desired outcomes. Moreover, sharing intentions creates a collective energy, allowing others to support, celebrate, and join forces in working towards shared goals.

To stay accountable and reinforce your commitment, consider practical steps like printing and laminating your intentions, placing them where you can see them daily (by your computer, in the car, or your wallet), and setting up rewards for repeating them daily for 21 days. Attach objects or images associated with your intentions, creating a tangible reminder of your journey. For instance, if your intention is to cultivate calmness, include a picture of yourself meditating or an image of something serene that resonates with you.

I AM: ________________________________

I AM: ________________________________

I AM: ________________________________

Embarking on a Journey of Self-Love and Gratitude

While the exploration of chakras and their role in weight loss may be your initial quest, the foundation of this journey lies in self-love and healing. Our bodies, intricate marvels of biology, tirelessly perform myriad functions each day without our explicit request. They beat, breathe, and sustain us in ways we often take for granted. Before delving into the specifics of chakra alignment for weight loss, it's essential to pause and express gratitude to the incredible vessel that carries us through life. Begin with love and thankfulness—acknowledge your heart's steady beat, your lungs' rhythmic breath, and the countless functions seamlessly orchestrated within. Starting with a foundation of love and gratitude is not just a choice; it's a powerful step towards holistic well-being.

Embark on Your Chakra Journey with Us!

Are you ready to unlock the secrets of your body's energy centers? Welcome to the transformative world of chakras, where mind, body, and spirit converge. At Wait Loss Journeys, we're here to guide you through the profound influence each chakra wields on your well-being. From the foundational Root Chakra, grounding you in stability, to the ethereal

Crown Chakra, connecting you to higher consciousness, each plays a unique role. If you're eager to delve deeper into the specifics or seek personalized insights, don't hesitate to reach out. Visit our website at waitlossjourneys.com or grab any of the amazing journals listed her: amazon. Your chakra journey begins here! We are currently working on mediations for each chakra when they are ready they will be available on debzng.com.

Should you decide to start on your own, that's amazing! On the next few pages you will find some ways to start with each chakra. Journaling and mediation is always a great place to start. Try to take a week for each one!

Embark on Your Root Chakra Journey!

Welcome to the foundational realm of the Root Chakra, the Muladhara, where the essence of grounding and stability takes root at the base of your spine. As the Earth element governs this

chakra, it intertwines with themes of support, structure, and prosperity. Here's your starting point: Begin with mindfulness during meals. Nourishing your body is an act of survival, and being present during this fundamental activity fosters a sense of grounding. This week's challenge is to confront fear—identify what you fear, understand its roots, and transform it into actionable steps. Triumph over charged situations, embrace mindful eating, and pamper your body with activities that enhance well-being. Affirm: "It is safe for me to be here. I love my body and trust its wisdom. I am IN here. The Earth supports me. I live in abundance. I hold my ground no matter what I encounter."
For those seeking deeper insights, contact us at waitlossjourneys.com.
Your Root Chakra journey starts now!

Dive into the Sacral Seas!

Embark on a journey to your Sacral Chakra, Svadhisthana, nestled in the abdomen between the navel and hip crease. As the element of

Water flows through this chakra, it invites you to explore sensation, emotion, and the exquisite dance of pleasure. The Sacral Chakra's purpose is to amplify your capacity for joy and movement. Your skill set: Tune into the charge of your emotions. Feel their sensations, detach from the stories, and let your body release and harvest their energy. This week, indulge in pleasure. Schedule something delightful, savoring every moment—a dinner, a serene bath, or a captivating date night. Triumph as your hips move with ease, your sex life blossoms, and you become more attuned to your emotions. Affirm: "I deserve pleasure. I feel good. I embrace and celebrate my sexuality. It is safe to feel my emotions. I listen to my feelings. Life is pleasurable." For deeper insights, connect with us at waitlossjourneys.com.
Let the Sacral Chakra's currents carry you to newfound joys!

Ignite Your Inner Fire!

Enter the radiant realm of the Solar Plexus Chakra, Manipura, located at the solar plexus. This powerhouse of fire energy governs your metabolism, personal power, and will. The lustrous gem, Manipura, holds the key to strength, autonomy, and confidence. Empower yourself with the skill of changing your mental vocabulary—replace "I have to" with "I choose to." Your weekly challenge: Tackle a task you've been procrastinating, unlocking the gift of personal empowerment.
Triumph as you feel more powerful, accomplish tasks with ease, and experience a surge of energy. Affirm: "I honor the power within me. I follow through with my will. My inner fire burns through blocks and fears. My will and divine will are aligned. I know my purpose. I do it easily and effortlessly." For deeper insights and to stoke the flames of empowerment, connect with us at waitlossjourneys.com .
Let the Solar Plexus Chakra illuminate your path to unwavering strength and confidence!

Embrace the Power of Love!

Step into the heart-centered domain of the Heart Chakra, Anahata, residing in the center of your chest. Like a gentle breeze, this chakra is associated with the element of Air, fostering love, compassion, and balance. Anahata, meaning 'unhurt, unstruck, and unbeaten,' invites you to face the challenge of working through grief and, in return, offers the gift of a light heart filled with love.

Master the skill of choosing understanding over judgment as you navigate life's intricate tapestry. Your weekly challenge: Cultivate gratitude by adding one thing to your list each day for a week. Affirm: "I am worthy of love. I love easily. I hold myself and others in compassion. There is an infinite supply of love. Love is my natural state of being. I live in balance with others."

Triumph as you experience more self-love and acceptance, a deeper connection with others, and a gentle, soothing presence within your body. For a journey into the heart's profound

realms, connect with us at waitlossjourneys.com
.

Let the Heart Chakra be your guide to a life brimming with love and harmony!

Unleash Your True Voice!

Embark on a journey through the ethereal realms of the Throat Chakra, Vissudha, nestled in your throat. Governed by the element of Ether, this chakra resonates with sound, vibration, and the purifying essence of truthful expression. Vissudha, meaning 'purification,' serves as a bridge to harmonize body, mind, and spirit through authentic communication. Hone the skill of self-awareness in communication—notice when you choose silence, explore the reasons, and feel its impact on your body. Your weekly challenge: Speak your withholds, clearing the path for genuine connection. Affirm: "I can speak my truth. My voice is necessary. My truth matters. I listen deeply to others. Creativity flows through me. I live in harmony."

Triumph as you experience the liberating feeling of clarity in communication, forging deeper connections with others and fostering mutual understanding. For an exploration into the transformative power of your voice, reach out to us at waitlossjourneys.com.

Let the Throat Chakra be your guide to authentic expression and harmonious living!

Awaken Your Inner Sight!

Venture into the realm of the Third Eye Chakra, Ajna, nestled between your brows. Governed by the element of Light, Ajna invites you to perceive and command, unlocking the powers of intuition, imagination, and vision.

Embrace the skill of choosing to see the positive—shift from the habitual focus on negativity to a holistic perspective of truth.

Your weekly challenge: Pierce through illusion and see beauty, manifesting external harmony.

Affirm: "I see with clarity. I pay attention to my intuition. I have a vision. I focus my attention to see clearly. I value my insights. I am open to the wisdom within."

Triumph as you cultivate intuition and envision a brighter reality. Explore the beauty around you, and let the Third Eye guide you to a world of clarity and insight. For deeper insights into your inner vision, connect with us at waitlossjourneys.com . Let Ajna be your beacon, illuminating the path to inner wisdom and heightened perception!

Embrace Divine Unity with Sahasrara!

Step into the realm of the Crown Chakra, Sahasrara, your cosmic connection to transcendent wisdom and unity. Located at the cerebral cortex, it is the pinnacle of consciousness, representing the order and meaning underlying existence.

Cultivate the skill of being in your witness, a state of mindful observation detached from judgment or attachment. This week's challenge: Meditate for 10 minutes daily, fostering awareness of your body, consciousness, and the unity that surrounds you. Affirm: "I am awake and aware. The world is my teacher. I am guided by higher intelligence. I am guided by inner wisdom. Divinity resides within. All is one." Triumph as you develop witness consciousness, releasing attachments and fully embracing the present moment. Connect with us at waitlossjourneys.com to explore the transformative power of Sahasrara.

Awaken to the divine essence within and unite with the universal wisdom that flows through every fiber of your being.

When your chakras are feeling clear and unblocked you can begin the manifesting currents of whatever you need or want or desire. Doing a chakra dive means checking your chakras for blocks and then opening up your manifesting currents, let's go deeper.

Chakra Dive 🌈✨

Hey there, cosmic explorers! 🚀 Let's take a joyride through the magical realms of Chakras! 🌀✨

In the cosmic dictionary, 'Chakra' translates to 'wheel' or 'disk' in Sanskrit – your personal energy hubs! 🌌 For eons, these bad boys have been the rockstars of spiritual practices, weaving their mojo into our very existence.

Why bother, you ask? Well, tuning into these energy epicenters isn't just about achieving mystical vibes; it's your backstage pass to boosting your life span and leveling up your physical, mental, and emotional game. 🚀 💪

Imagine this: you, fully synced with your body and mind, cruising through the cosmos of your own existence. 🌌 🚀 But beware! Blocked or wonky chakras are like cosmic traffic jams, slowing down your life force and messing with your groove. 😩

Fear not! Enter the realm of chakra alignment – the Jedi training for your soul. 🌈 ✨ Becoming the Yoda of your chakras means you can declutter your mind, vibe with the universe, and basically become the superhero of your story. 💫 💪

Now, if your chakras are feeling a bit wonky, fear not! We've got the ultimate sidekicks: Aromatherapy and Crystals! 🌿 💎 These bad boys are like the Batman and Robin of the energy world, swooping in to balance and cleanse your chakras.
But wait, there's more! Yoga, the superhero workout for your soul. 🧘 ✨ It's the life force

energy pumping through your veins, doing somersaults and cartwheels to keep those chakra points lit. When energy gets stuck, cue the superhero soundtrack – anxiety, lethargy, wonky digestion. Yoga is here to save the day, moving that energy like a boss.

So, fellow cosmic crusaders, gear up! 🚀🌌 Tune in, chill out, and let the energy flow. Your chakras will thank you, and the universe will high-five you for being the rockstar of your own cosmic show! 🌟✌️ #ChakraMagic #EnergyAlignment #CosmicAdventure

Unlocking the Power Within: The Dance of Liberation and Manifestation

In the cosmic dance of energy within us, there exists a profound journey—from the rooted depths of the chakras to the expansive realms of manifestation. This journey, defined by the liberating and manifesting currents, is a roadmap to not just weight loss but to the manifestation of your deepest desires, be it radiant health, abundance, love, or more.

The Liberator: Unleashing the Upward Current

Imagine a river flowing from the very roots of your being, ascending through the chakras like a liberating current. This is the force that seeks freedom, expansion, and universality—the upward pull of mind and spirit. It begins at the foundational root chakra, where you confront the roots of limitations. Here, in the raw energy of survival, lies the genesis of blockages that hinder your journey to manifestation.

As you traverse this upward current, you liberate yourself. The sacral chakra dances with the freeing energy of creativity and pleasure, breaking through constraints. The solar plexus chakra ignites the fire of personal power, burning away self-imposed limitations. The heart chakra, the bridge between earthly and spiritual realms, opens wide, releasing the constraints that bind love.

The liberating current ascends further, reaching the expressive throat chakra, where your voice is freed from the shackles of silence. The intuitive third eye chakra unfolds, granting clarity beyond the veils of illusion. Finally, the crown chakra, your connection to the divine, emerges as the pinnacle, liberating your spirit to transcend earthly limits.

The Manifestor: Crafting the Downward Flow

Having traversed the liberating current, you stand at the precipice of manifestation. The manifesting current, the pull of the soul and body, propels you downward, guiding your intentions into the material world.

Begin at the crown chakra, the seat of cosmic consciousness. Here, your desires, now liberated from limitations, take form. The third eye chakra visualizes these desires, shaping them with clarity and purpose. The throat chakra breathes life into your intentions, giving them a voice.

Descend to the heart chakra, where the essence of love infuses your desires with pure intention. The solar plexus chakra lends the power of personal will, grounding your aspirations in determination. The sacral chakra, the creative center, molds your intentions with the passion of creation.

Finally, arrive at the root chakra, the anchor to earthly existence. Here, your desires take root in the material world, forming the boundaries and individuality that shape your reality.

Embrace the Dance: Liberation and Manifestation Unite

In this cosmic ballet of energy, the liberating and manifesting currents converge. The dance from root to crown and back down is a symphony of transformation—a journey of self-discovery, release, and creation.

As you delve into the depths of your being, confronting and liberating yourself from the blocks that bind, you pave the way for manifestation. The upward and downward currents intertwine, creating a harmonious flow where the mind, spirit, and body unite in the alchemy of creation.

This is the essence of your power—to liberate and manifest, to transcend and shape your reality. As you embark on this profound journey, remember: the dance of liberation and manifestation is the dance of your soul, a dance of limitless possibilities waiting to unfold.

Are you ready to embrace the rhythm and manifest the life you envision?
If so, read on for some even deeper methods and some information on auras and how they are connected to chakras.

Chakra Alchemy: Crystal Grids and Harmonious Practices 🌈💎

In the mystical realm of chakras, crystal grids emerge as enchanting allies, magnifying and focusing intent. Let's unravel the secrets of this sacred dance:

Crystal Grid Mastery - Threefold Path:

Intent - The Blueprint of Manifestation: To embark on the crystal grid journey, clarity of intent is paramount. Define your desires and articulate success in your terms. Like an architect with a blueprint, the intent becomes the guiding force shaping the energy.

Open to Receive - Synchronicities and Serendipities: As the grid takes form, open your heart and mind to receive the energy, guidance, and healing it offers. Witness synchronicities and serendipities as signs that the universe is responding to your intent. This is the dance of receptivity, a cosmic dialogue.

Taking Action - The Physical Symphony: The magic of the grid unfolds not just in the metaphysical but in the physical realm. Be ready for action, the tangible steps that align with your intent. Shifts will occur, and with preparedness, you step into the transformation, shaping the energy into reality.

Loving Kindness Meditation - An Offering of Light: In the practice of Loving Kindness, a beacon of compassion, envision faces in your mind:

- Someone you adore.
- Someone you respect.
- Someone you are neutral towards.
- Someone you don't like. For each, repeat the mantra: "May they be healthy, may they be happy, and may they be free from suffering." This meditation, a gift of light, dissolves resentment and negativity, fostering a garden of loving-kindness.

Color Breathing Activity - Inhaling Vibrant Energy: Choose a color aligned with the chakra you seek to balance. Close your eyes, breathe in the chosen color, envisioning it spreading through every fiber of your being. Notice the sensations, immerse in the hues. Open your eyes, grounding yourself in the present. A breath of vibrancy, a dance of equilibrium.

Balancing the Chakras Activity - Flame Meditation: Sit comfortably, gaze at a candle flame, and let stillness engulf you. Watch the flame without blinking, absorbing its dance. Close your eyes, observe the residual image until it fades. Open your eyes, repeat, or take a deep breath to conclude. A dance with the flame, a meditation in balance.

Grounding the Chakras - Dance of Harmony: Music, the expression of the soul, harmonizes with dance, a recharge for the chakras. Dance freely, releasing the inner self. Let the rhythm guide, unburdened by external thoughts. After this dance of liberation, lie down, and bask in the harmony that dances within.
In this symphony of practices, from crystal grids to loving-kindness, color breathing, and the dance of harmony, the chakras find their rhythm, a dance of energies merging with the

cosmic flow. 🌌 💃 #ChakraHarmony #CrystalAlchemy #SoulfulDance

The Energetic Tapestry: Auras and Chakras Unveiled

In the vibrant tapestry of human energy, each one of us is surrounded by an aura—an ethereal glow that reflects the essence of our being. This luminous field extends beyond the physical body, pulsating with colors and frequencies that encode the stories of our emotions, thoughts, and spiritual well-being.

Understanding Auras: Windows to the Soul

Imagine your aura as a kaleidoscope of hues, each color representing a unique aspect of your consciousness. Auras are not just a visual spectacle for those with a special gift; they are a dynamic expression of the energy centers within us—our chakras. These spinning wheels of energy, aligned along the spine, are the gatekeepers of our life force.

Aura-Chakra Symbiosis: The Dance of Energy

Your aura and chakras share an intimate dance, interweaving their energies to create a harmonious symphony. The colors of your aura often correspond to the state of your chakras. For instance, a vibrant, balanced aura might signify aligned and open chakras, while a clouded or erratic aura could indicate blockages or imbalances within your energy centers.

Chakra Harmony: Radiance in Every Hue

Delve into the chakra system, and you'll discover that each chakra resonates with a specific color and energy frequency. The root chakra, positioned at the base of the spine, is often associated with red energy. As you ascend through the chakras, the colors transition through the spectrum, reaching the crown chakra at the top of the head, bathed in violet or white light.

When your chakras are in harmony, this radiant energy translates into a vibrant and cohesive aura. Picture a balanced heart chakra infusing your aura with shades of green, signifying compassion and love. Conversely, a blockage in this heart-centered energy might cast a shadow over your aura, revealing the need for healing and restoration.

Embracing the Aura's Wisdom

Your aura is not just a visual spectacle; it's a dynamic feedback system, offering insights into your emotional, mental, and spiritual states. By tuning into the colors and patterns of your aura, you gain a window into your inner world—a powerful tool for self-awareness and growth.

In the journey of holistic well-being, understanding the dance between your aura and chakras becomes a roadmap. As you nurture and balance your chakras, you cultivate a radiant and harmonious aura—a testament to the interconnected dance of energy that defines your vibrant existence.

The Root Chakra: Gateway to Vitality and Power

At the very base of our energetic system lies the root chakra, an essential center pulsating with the primal force of life. This foundational energy hub is intimately connected with the color red—a hue that mirrors the lifeblood coursing through our veins. As we explore the realms of the aura, we discover that this crimson energy extends to the innermost layer—a vibrant echo of our inherent vitality.

Root Chakra Aura: The Scarlet Symphony of Action and Courage

Picture your aura resonating with the vibrant shades of scarlet or ruby—a clear, bright red that encapsulates the essence of the root chakra. This dynamic interplay signifies a life force teeming with action, survival instincts, and an unyielding determination to overcome obstacles. In the language of colors, this vivid red palette is an ode to courage, passion, and the physical energy that propels us forward on our journey.

However, like any masterpiece, nuances weave through this scarlet symphony. A red aura can be a double-edged sword, revealing not only a zest for life but also potential challenges. A clear and bright red hue may signal an individual capable of triumphing over adversities, showcasing resilience and a vibrant approach to life. Yet, it may also whisper of a short temper or tendencies towards assertiveness bordering on bullying.

The Archangel of the Scarlet Realm: Camael, Rider of Victory

As we delve into the metaphysical guardianship of the root chakra and its red aura, we encounter the archangel Camael. This celestial being, the archangel of Mars, gracefully guides us through the realms of power, change, and victory. Picture Camael astride his leopard, an emblem of triumph and ferocity. In the dance of energies, he becomes the guiding force, steering us towards the victorious realization of our desires.

As you engage with the root chakra's red aura, envision Camael riding alongside, urging you to embrace your inner strength, overcome challenges, and manifest your destiny. This archangelic presence serves as a beacon of courage, a reminder that within the scarlet hues of your aura lies the power to conquer, transform, and emerge victorious in the grand tapestry of life.

In the symphony of colors and energies, the root chakra, its scarlet aura, and the watchful gaze of Archangel Camael entwine—a manifestation of the cosmic dance within, inviting you to embark on a journey of courage, resilience, and triumphant transformation.

The Sacral Chakra: Embracing the Radiance of Orange

In the energetic kaleidoscope of our being, the sacral chakra emerges as the radiant core of confidence, independence, and a strong sense of identity. As we venture into the expansive realms of the aura, the second layer unfolds—a luminous orange canvas pulsating with the hues of integration and personal empowerment.

Sacral Chakra Aura: The Dance of Confidence and Creativity

Visualize your aura adorned in rich hues of orange, a testament to the integrator that is the sacral chakra. This vibrant layer, extending outward from the body, signifies confidence, fertility, and a flourishing sense of self-esteem. A positive, rich orange aura becomes a tapestry of integration—where different aspects of life seamlessly coalesce.

In this radiant spectrum, rich orange becomes the symbol of social prowess, self-motivation, originality, and creative abilities. It speaks of a harmonious dance of energies, where the individual integrates diverse facets of life with grace and authenticity. For those yearning to expand their families, bright orange becomes a beacon of hope, fostering fertility and the fulfillment of personal desires.

The Archangel of the Orange Radiance: Gabriel, Archangel of the Moon

As we traverse the sacral chakra's vibrant landscape, we encounter the celestial guardian—Archangel Gabriel, the archangel of the moon. Envision Gabriel's luminous presence, weaving through the orange hues, guiding you towards a harmonious integration of emotions, desires, and creative energies. In the dance of the sacral chakra, Gabriel becomes the gentle force, nurturing the seeds of confidence and independence.

However, within this luminosity lies the subtle dance of shadows—a spectrum of negative qualities that may manifest. A pale or murky orange aura hints at a lack of identity or low self-esteem, echoing concerns about external perceptions. An overly harsh orange, verging on excesses and obsessions, may signify challenges, especially in areas related to food and self-image.

In the enchanting interplay of the sacral chakra, its orange aura, and the guidance of Archangel Gabriel, discover a profound journey towards confidence, creativity, and the harmonious integration of your radiant identity.

The Solar Plexus Chakra: Illuminating Paths with Yellow Radiance

Embark on a journey through the vibrant spectrum of the solar plexus chakra—a realm where logic, intellectual achievement, and versatility converge. As we extend our gaze to the third layer of the aura, a luminous yellow unfolds, becoming a beacon for communicators and travelers alike.

Solar Plexus Chakra Aura: The Brilliance of Logic and Versatility

Imagine your aura aglow in the hues of clear lemon, embodying a focused mind, a sharp memory, and financial clarity. Yellow, the color of the communicator and traveler, becomes the third level of the aura—a layer intricately woven into the fabric of everyday living. Positive qualities of this radiant yellow spectrum include a joyful vibrancy and clear communication.

A bright canary yellow aura becomes the signature of joy and eloquent expression—akin to the brilliance of an actor or entertainer on stage. Yet, within this luminosity exists the subtle dance of shadows. Irregular, harsh streaks of yellow may signify hyperactivity, while mustard yellow may mask emotions of jealousy or resentment. Metallic yellow, with its undertones of less-than-honest intent, may point to tendencies towards gambling.

The Archangel of the Yellow Radiance: Raphael,
Archangel of Healing and Travel
As we traverse the luminous expanse of the
solar plexus chakra's yellow aura, we encounter
the celestial guide—Archangel Raphael, the
archangel of healing, travel, and the
entrepreneur. Picture Raphael's benevolent
presence, infusing your yellow aura with healing
vibrations, guiding your intellectual pursuits,
and lighting the path for transformative
journeys.

Within this brilliant tapestry, variations in yellow
carry nuanced messages. A sharp yellow may
denote logical thinking with a touch of sarcasm,
while a cold yellow may signal a mind ruling
over the heart.

In the symphony of the solar plexus chakra, its
yellow aura, and the gentle guidance of
Archangel Raphael, discover a luminous
journey toward intellectual prowess, versatile
communication, and transformative
exploration.

The Heart Chakra: Nurturing Love in the Lush Green Aura

Step into the enchanting realm of the heart chakra—a sacred space resonating with love, trust, and the harmonious growth of natural energies. As we venture into the fourth layer of the aura, an ethereal green unfolds, a testament to the compassionate heart and guardian of the environment.

Heart Chakra Aura: The Verdant Symphony of Love and Trust

Envision your aura bathed in the rich hues of clear green—a visual poem of fidelity, trust, and the natural harmony of growth. Green, the color of the child of nature, becomes the fourth layer of the aura—an outermost daily life level that, at its limits, reflects a profound love for humanity.

A positive, rich, and clear green aura becomes the signature of a trustworthy, loving heart—one who generously shares time, love, and resources, and whose words resonate from the depths of sincerity. This vibrant green palette is the mark of an individual deeply committed to the art of love, where emerald green unveils the essence of a natural healer, particularly in the alternative healing field, and a soul marked by fortune.

The Archangel of the Green Haven: Anael, Archangel of Lasting Love

As we immerse ourselves in the lush green expanse of the heart chakra's aura, we encounter the celestial custodian—Archangel Anael, the archangel of lasting love, fidelity, and natural growth in all matters. Picture Anael's gentle presence, infusing your green aura with the enduring vibrations of love, trust, and a commitment to the flourishing tapestry of life.

Yet, within this verdant sanctuary, shadows may cast their subtle dance. A pale green aura may hint at emotional dependency, while a dull or muddy green may signify conflicting emotions or an energy vampire draining the life force. Yellow-green may point to possessiveness, and lime green could signal stress in current relationships. Dark or olive green may reveal a propensity to love unwisely.

In the symphony of the heart chakra, its green aura, and the nurturing guidance of Archangel Anael, discover an immersive journey into the realms of enduring love, trust, and the flourishing tapestry of natural growth.

The Throat Chakra: Unveiling Truth in the Soothing Blue Aura

Embark on a journey into the expansive realms of the throat chakra—a luminous sanctuary of ideals, broad vision, and the transmission of healing powers from higher sources. As we delve into the fifth layer of the aura, an ethereal blue unfolds, a reflection of the seeker of truth and the first of the higher and outer aura levels.

Throat Chakra Aura: The Majestic Hue of Truth and Leadership

Visualize your aura adorned in the regal hues of royal blue—a symbol of an integrated personality, a keen sense of justice, and the natural powers of leadership. Blue, the color of the seeker of truth, becomes the fifth layer of the aura—an outermost expanse that holds the potential for a broadened perspective and the embodiment of natural authority.

Positive qualities of this majestic blue spectrum include bright blue—a testament to creativity and altruism. Pale blue becomes the signature of the idealist, boasting a global vision. Clear blue radiates objectivity, transforming its bearer into a gifted speaker and teacher. Blue auras suffusing other colors often grace the presence of spiritual healers, authors, musicians, actors, and other performers.

The Archangel of the Azure Vistas: Sachiel, Archangel of Harvest and Truth

As we immerse ourselves in the soothing blue of the throat chakra's aura, we encounter the celestial guardian—Archangel Sachiel, the archangel of the harvest, truth, justice, prosperity, and expansion in every realm of learning. Picture Sachiel's benevolent presence, infusing your blue aura with the vibrations of truth, justice, and the expansive tapestry of prosperity.

Yet, within this azure sanctuary, shadows may cast their nuanced dance. A dull, dense blue may signal increased conservatism and rigid rule-keeping, while harsh blue may manifest as autocratic, opinionated, and judgmental.

In the symphony of the throat chakra, its blue aura, and the nurturing guidance of Archangel Sachiel, discover a journey into the realms of truth, justice, and the expansive horizons of leadership.

The Third Eye Chakra: Navigating the Depths of Indigo Insight

Embark on a mystical journey through the realms of the third eye chakra—a sacred space resonating with inner vision, psychic awareness, and the profound knowledge of past lives and worlds. As we explore the sixth layer of the aura, an ethereal indigo unfolds, a manifestation of the seer, the wise one, and the evolving soul.

Third Eye Chakra Aura: The Enigmatic Shades of Indigo Wisdom

Picture your aura bathed in the enigmatic shades of clear indigo—a canvas alive with acute sensitivity to unspoken intentions, an awareness of the spiritual world, and an enhanced intuition that dances between clairvoyance and clairaudience. Indigo, the color of the seer, becomes the second of the higher aura levels and the sixth layer moving outward from the body—a bridge between the tangible and the ethereal.

Positive qualities of this indigo spectrum include bright shades indicating a fertile imagination and deep indigo gracing the auras of wise older individuals. Lavender, a related shade, brings sensitivity to higher powers within nature, granting those with a lavender tinge an awareness of angels and gifts for herbalism.

The Archangel of Indigo Insight: Cassiel, Archangel of Consolation

As we traverse the depths of indigo insight, we encounter the celestial consoler—Archangel Cassiel, the archangel of consolation and compassion for the world's sorrows. Visualize Cassiel's comforting presence, infusing your indigo aura with the vibrations of solace, joy, and acceptance of what cannot be changed.

Yet, within this mystical indigo tapestry, shadows may weave their subtle dance. A blurred indigo may imply spending too long on daydreams or absorbing others' bad moods and stress. A dark indigo may signal isolation and disillusionment.

In the symphony of the third eye chakra, its indigo aura, and the comforting embrace of Archangel Cassiel, discover a journey into the depths of wisdom, psychic awareness, and the consoling power of compassionate insight.

The Crown Chakra: Merging with Cosmic Energies in Violet Splendor

Embark on the final frontier of spiritual exploration—the crown chakra—a radiant haven resonating with violet splendor, medium senses, and a profound connection with other dimensions, ancestors, angels, and spirit guides. This ethereal violet unfolds as the color of the mystic, the visionary, and the integration between all aspects of the self and the spiritual world.

Crown Chakra Aura: The Ethereal Dance of Violet Wisdom

Imagine your aura bathed in the ethereal dance of violet—a testimony to medium senses, connection with other dimensions, and a sacred communion with ancestors and celestial beings. Violet, the color of the mystic, becomes the highest aura level, merging into white and gold as it joins with pure cosmic energies.

Positive qualities of this radiant violet spectrum include a connection with unconscious wisdom, lateral and global thinking, and the ability to disregard immediate gain for long-term goals. A vibrant violet aura embodies love and tolerance for humanity, peacemaking with the highest ethics, and the ability to heal through higher energy sources like angels and wise guides.

The Archangel of Violet Wisdom: Zadkiel, Archangel of Truth and Justice
As we immerse ourselves in the splendor of violet wisdom, we encounter the celestial guide—Archangel Zadkiel, the archangel of truth and justice, higher healing, abundance,

the performing arts, alternative therapies, and major charitable initiatives. Picture Zadkiel's benevolent presence, infusing your violet aura with the vibrations of truth, justice, and the boundless potential for higher healing.

Yet, within this mystical violet tapestry, shadows may cast their nuanced dance. A too-pale violet may signify a lack of drive, incentive, and stamina, while a harsh and unrealistic shade may indicate grand plans that do not come to fruition. Dull violet may hint at feelings of depression.

For those with white in the crown chakra, it signifies limitless potential, boundless energy, and the free-flowing life force—the color of the soaring spirit, the quester, and the innovator. This vibrant white can form the top of the outermost layer in highly evolved individuals, especially where indigo and violet merge. Positive qualities of this vibrant white spectrum include the aura of those who follow a unique life path and make a difference in the world, drawing pure, undiffused light from the cosmos for healing.

Archangels of Synthesis: Michael and Gabriel

Archangel Michael, the archangel of the sun, and Archangel Gabriel, the archangel of the moon, represent the synthesis of outer and inner worlds. Michael, with a male focus, and Gabriel, with a female focus, embody the unity of male and female energies.

The crown chakra extends from the center of the hairline on the upper forehead to about an inch above the head, where it merges with the minor yet significant soul star chakra, containing the unchanging divine spark of our evolved or higher spiritual self.

In the symphony of the crown chakra, its violet aura, and the celestial embrace of Archangel Zadkiel, discover a journey into the realms of cosmic connection, boundless wisdom, and the eternal dance of the soul.

Closing: Nurturing Your Radiant Aura and Balanced Chakras

As we conclude our exploration into the vibrant tapestry of auras and chakras, consider the profound wisdom that lies within the hues of your energetic field. A glimpse into your aura, captured in a picture, can be a potent mirror reflecting the current state of your chakras. It unveils the dance of energies—positive and negative—allowing you to focus your attention on areas that may benefit from nurturing and healing.

Obtaining an aura picture becomes a tangible gateway to understanding which chakras are functioning positively, radiating vibrant energies, and which may require your tender care and attention. It is an insightful tool guiding you on your journey towards holistic well-being.

Embrace the notion that cleansing your aura is a sacred practice, a renewal of your energetic essence that resonates deeply with the health of your chakras. Nature becomes a potent ally in this endeavor—immerse yourself in the soothing embrace of the outdoors. Let the cleansing waters of the ocean or any natural body of water wash away stagnant energies, leaving you refreshed and revitalized.

Explore the transformative power of crystals, engage in meditative practices, and let the rhythmic waves of deep breathing harmonize your internal energies. The ancient art of smudging with sage or other sacred herbs can purify your energetic field, while the gentle glow of candles infuses your aura with a calming radiance.

In your quest for a vibrant aura and balanced chakras, remember that the simplicity of daily rituals holds immeasurable power. Let the healing energies of these practices ripple through your being, fostering a harmonious dance between your physical, emotional, and spiritual realms.

May your aura shine brightly, a reflection of the balanced and nourished chakras within. As you continue your journey of self-discovery and healing, may each step be guided by the profound wisdom of your radiant energies.

Embrace the luminosity within, and let the vibrant dance of your aura and chakras unfold in harmony with the symphony of the universe.

Colors are also important in Auras and Chakras:

Harmony of Colors and Elements in the Tapestry of Healing 🌈✨

In the canvas of healing and spiritual exploration, colors emerge as potent symbols, each carrying its own unique energy and significance. Let's unravel the threads of this vibrant tapestry:

White - The Calm Spirit: In the pureness of white, all colors converge. It is the embodiment of calmness, clarity, and a beacon that shines with the essence of teaching and perfection. A canvas awaiting the strokes of wisdom to be painted.

Black - The Discrete Protector: Black, the guardian of all colors, stands as a discreet and protective force. It retains the spectrum within its depths, a shield against external energies. In

its quietude, it holds the power to safeguard
and ground.

Healing Energy - The Journey Inward: The
healing journey unfolds in stages: first love,
self-love, and the pursuit of non-attachment.
The energy of right intention, the third stage,
becomes the compass guiding this
transformative odyssey.

Five Elements - The Sacred Symphony:
- Sacred Sound/Ether: Resonating with the
  liver, clear quartz, green tourmaline,
  bloodstone, green jasper, and labradorite
  compose the symphony of ether. The
  notes of clarity and healing echo through
  this ethereal realm.
- Fire: Igniting the heart, the fire element
  breathes life into energy. Fire opal,
  garnet, and ruby dance in this vibrant
  blaze, infusing vitality into the spirit.
- Earth: Nestled in the abdomen, the earth
  element cradles the immune system.
  Agates, black stones, citrines, and

carnelian form a grounding foundation, nurturing the body's resilient essence.
- Wind: Riding on the currents of thoughts and voice, the wind element whispers through white stones like opal, moonstone, and pearl, shaping the melodies of expression.
- Water: Flowing through the kidneys, the water element serenades with celestites, aquamarine, and opal, a gentle cascade of healing energies.

Blue, Red, and Yellow - The Laws of Manifestation:
- Blue: The will to live in the physical body unfolds in the serene blue. It is the hue of determination, embodying the vitality to navigate the earthly journey.
- Red: Love and compassion, the soul's devotion, find expression in the passionate red. It aligns the soul with intention, weaving a tapestry of heartfelt coherence.

- Yellow: Spirit and creative intelligence meld in the golden glow of yellow. It is the essence of the mind's brilliance and the creative spark that ignites the journey.

Warm, Neutral, and Cool Tones - The Temperature of Healing:
- Warm Tones (Red/Orange/Yellow): Infused with warmth, these tones foster long-term healing. They cradle the spirit in a comforting embrace, promoting sustained well-being.
- Neutral (Green): Green, the balancer, brings equilibrium and stability. It is the smooth vitality that energizes without overwhelming, a neutral haven for rejuvenation.
- Cool Tones (Blue/Indigo/Violet): Cool tones, like a gentle breeze, are linked with quick, sudden healing. They embody the essence of swiftness and serenity, guiding the spirit through moments of rapid transformation.

In this spectrum of colors and elements, the tapestry of healing and spiritual evolution unfurls, inviting us to explore the rich nuances and energies that dance within and around us. 

Closing

Embark on a transformative journey of self-love, gratitude, growth, and healing as you delve into the pages of "Chakras and Weight Loss." In this thought-provoking exploration, we've unraveled the profound connection between chakras and your well-being, offering a beginning roadmap to holistic transformation.

Beginning with the foundational Root Chakra, ground yourself in mindfulness, savoring each bite as a celebration of life. The Sacral Chakra awakens your senses, inviting pleasure and emotional charge into your daily existence. Moving to the Solar Plexus, you harness personal power, accomplishing tasks with newfound energy and confidence.

As we ascended to the Heart Chakra, embrace love and compassion, working through grief to cultivate a light heart. The Throat Chakra empowers you to speak your truth, fostering clear communication and creativity. The Third Eye guides you to see the positive, piercing through illusion to behold the beauty within.

Culminating in the Crown Chakra, you can experience divine unity, transcending the self to connect with the higher intelligence that guides your path.

Now, as you stand at the precipice of your own transformation, let the love and gratitude flow within yourself. Capture the essence of these chakras and begin where it will help you heal most first. Remember to start slow, pick something not too far off, set goals for yourself, write those positive affirmations, say them out loud every day and find some time to meditate. Embrace the wisdom of your journey, the power of self-love, and the beauty of healing. May this short ebook be a compass, guiding you towards a life of balance, joy, and profound well-being. Embark on your path with gratitude, for in this journey, you are not alone, and every step is a celebration of your divine essence.

OTHER BOOKS BY DEBBY NG:

Love Across Lifetimes: Raphaella & Octavio's Eternal Connection

MOONLIT REFLECTIONS: 2024 MOON JOURNAL

PRETTY GIRLS LOVE BAD BOYS: **REAL TALK**

PRETTY GIRLS LOVE BAD BOYS: **FRONT STREET**

PRETTY GIRLS LOVE BAD BOYS: **ROCKY RELATIONSHIPS**

ETHEREAL BONDS: UNRAVELING DIMENSIONS OF FORGIVENESS

JOURNALS - Check my Amazon Author Page for Details

Nurturing Minds, Building Futures: Cultivating Student-Teacher Relationships in Underserved Communities

"Unlocking Reading Success": Your Journey to Nurturing Lifelong Learners

www.ingramcontent.com/pod-product-compliance
Lightning Source LLC
Chambersburg PA
CBHW070816170726
48000CB00017B/926